# Learn dansk

# Danish

# for beginners

Christopher Panaretos
ISBN 9798842025985

# Table of Contents

# Tips for Language Learning

The most important thing is **self-esteem**. You must have self esteem above a certain threshold, otherwise your brain will prevent you from learning. You won't be aware of this effect, you will simply not feel motivated to learn.

Secondly, **practice** speaking, listening, writing, and reading for yourself. You only get better at something when you actually do it, not by reading or listening to someone describe how to do something.

Lastly, **time**. You should achieve a basic beginner level after about 250 hours. At 500 hours, have a solid beginner understanding. And at 1000 hours get to an intermediate level.

# Summary of Danish

# Universal Grammar Rules

The explanation of Danish presented in this book is based on an alternative, universal theory of grammar that is much different from traditional grammar, although there is overlap with some concepts. However, this alternative grammar theory is concise and provides a solid foundation for understanding how language works in general, so it is a good base for Danish-specific language rules to stand on.

The alternative grammar theory has five main concepts: thing, descriptor, scene, thing-converter, and scene-converter.

- **thing**: there are 6 categories of things in the world
  - object
  - concept
  - time
  - place
  - process
  - state

- **descriptor**: each of the six kinds of things can have its own properties unique to that thing, like color, size, or speed

- **scene**: a scene is a relative arrangement of things, where one of the things acts as a verb, another acts as subject, and 0, 1, or 2 other things are included depending on the type of scene; there are four types of scene
  - linking
  - intransitive
  - monotransitive
  - ditransitive

- **thing-converter**: these words turn a particular type of thing into one of the other six types of things, or into a descriptor

- **scene-converter**: these words turn a scene into a thing or into a descriptor

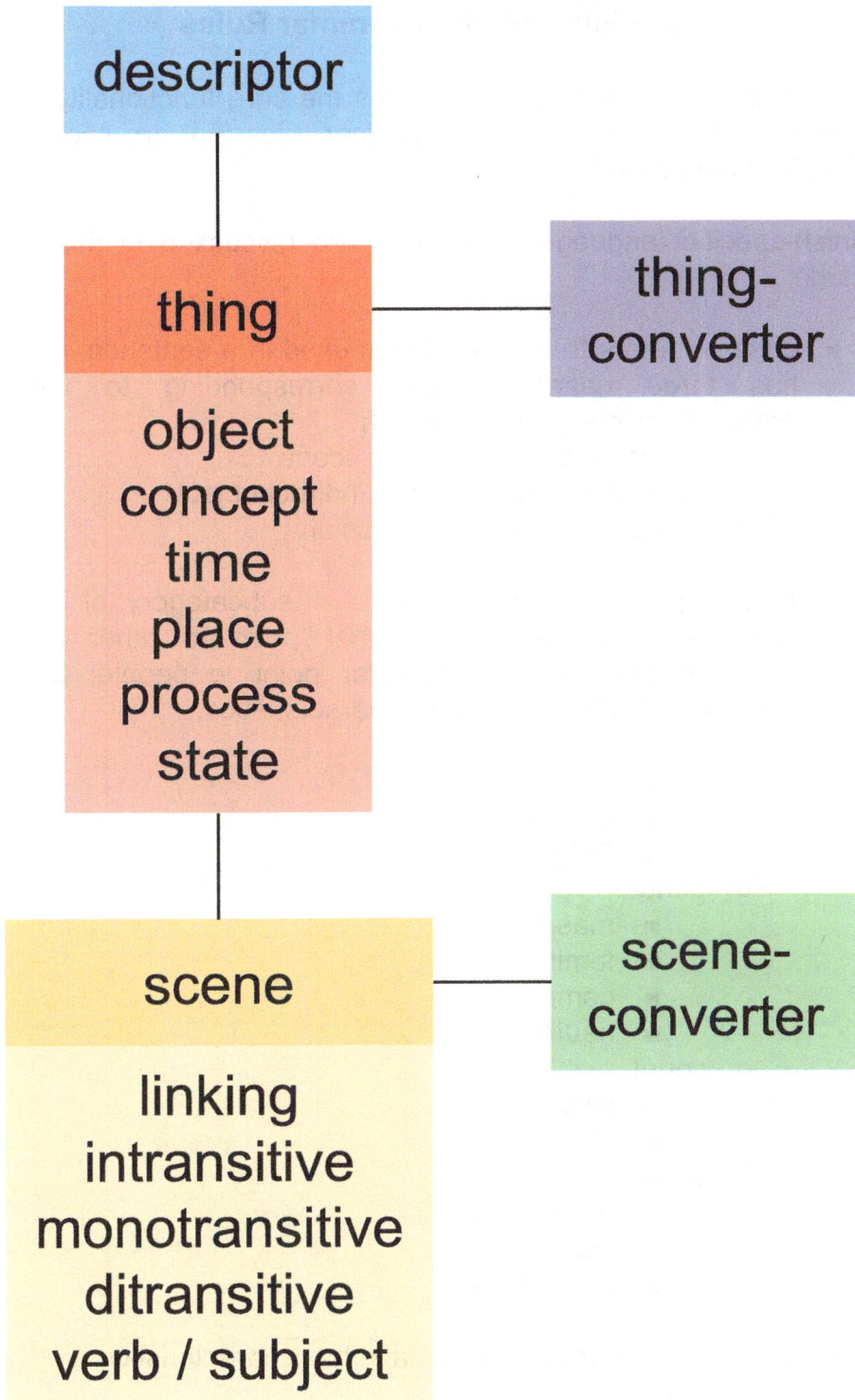

# Danish-Specific Grammar Rules

The grammar system above describes the core functionality of all languages. It does not include grammar rules that are specific to individual languages.

Danish-specific languages rules that are discussed in this book include:

- **case** → refers to how a thing is used in a sentence; Danish has three cases, *roughly* corresponding to various grammatical concepts in English
  - nominative :: subject of a scene
  - oblique :: direct object or indirect object
  - genitive :: to show possession

- **things::personal pronouns** → a subcategory of things, pronouns are placeholders that point to other things; personal pronouns in particular point to people; Danish personal pronouns have four characteristics…
  - perspective
    - 1st person
    - 2nd person
    - 3rd person
  - gender
    - masculine
    - feminine
    - common
    - neuter
  - count
    - singular
    - plural
  - case
    - nominative
    - oblique
    - possessive

- **things** → in Danish, things have two characteristics…
  - gender
    - common

- neuter
  - ○ count
    - ■ singular
    - ■ plural

- **descriptors::articles** → Danish includes two special subcategories of descriptors called definite articles and indefinite articles…
  - ○ definite articles indicate a particular instantiation of a thing, i.e. a specific item
  - ○ indefinite article indicates the presence of an item, but just one of a class, not a specific item in particular

- **descriptors** → Danish descriptors, including articles, exhibit target matching for three characteristics; they can change spelling to match their target's gender and count, and they can also change spelling depending on whether or not a definite article is associated with the target thing

- **verbs** → in Danish, verbs have three characteristics…
  - ○ mood
    - ■ indicative
    - ■ subjunctive
    - ■ imperative
  - ○ tense
    - ■ past
    - ■ present
    - ■ future
  - ○ aspect
    - ■ imperfect
    - ■ perfect

# Diagram of Danish-Specific Grammar Rules

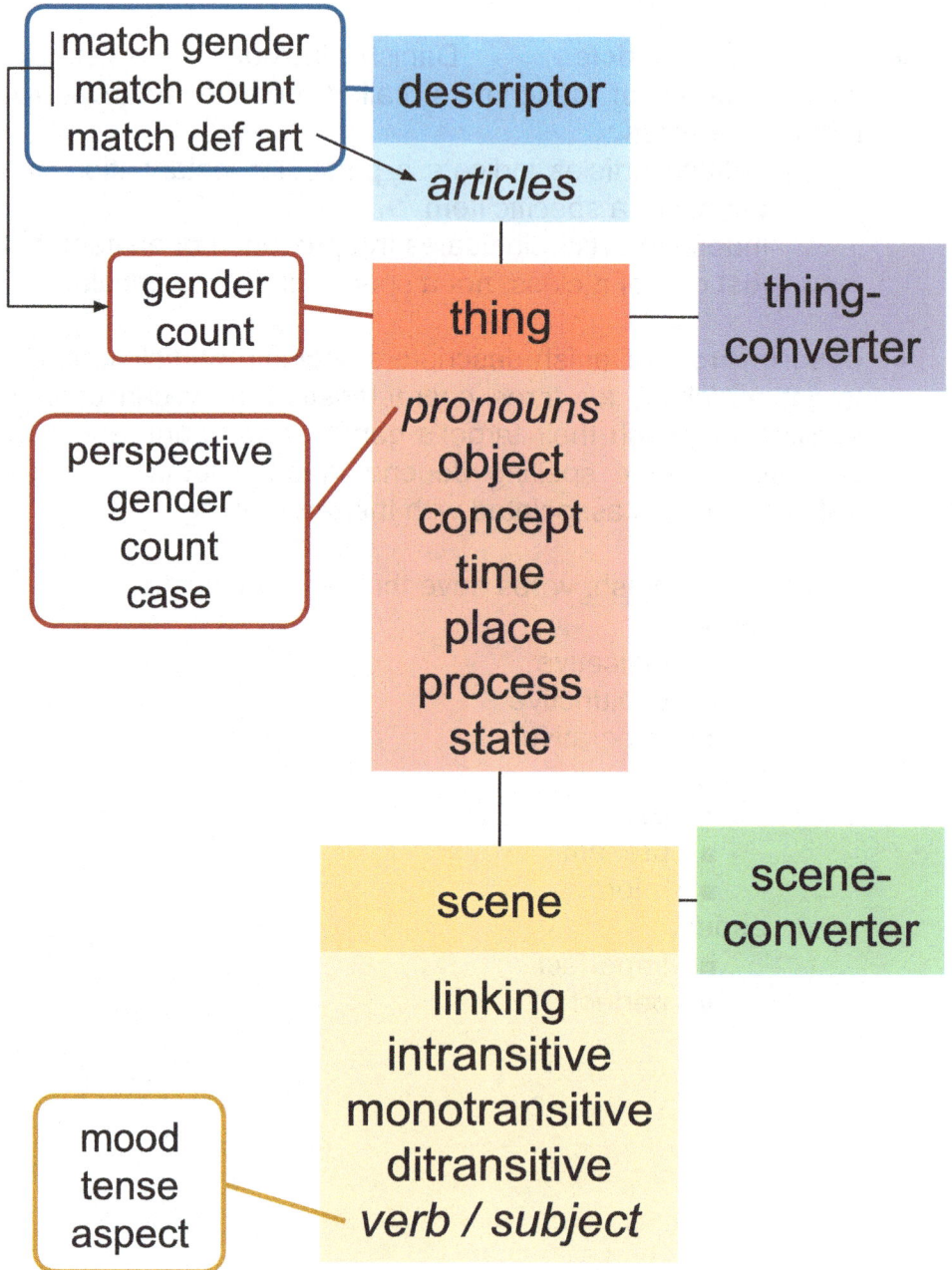

match gender
match count
match def art

**descriptor**

*articles*

gender
count

**thing**

**thing-converter**

perspective
gender
count
case

*pronouns*
object
concept
time
place
process
state

**scene**

**scene-converter**

linking
intransitive
monotransitive
ditransitive
*verb / subject*

mood
tense
aspect

# Spelling and Word Order

The grammar rules for Danish, as for all languages, can only be expressed in two fundamental ways: the spelling of each word, and the relative order of words. So for Danish, the question is how do the universal rules and the Danish-specific grammar rules manifest with respect to spelling and word order? Exploring this topic will be the focus of the rest of this book, but a summary is given here.

## Spelling

- **personal pronouns** change spelling depending on their *perspective*, *gender*, *count*, and *case*

- **things** change spelling depending on their *count*, and on which *article* is used, definite or indefinite

- **definite article** changes spelling to *match* its target thing's *gender* and *count*

- **indefinite article** changes spelling to *match* its target thing's *gender*

- **descriptors** change spelling to *match* their target thing's *gender* and *count*, and depending on whether the target uses a *definite article* or not

- **verbs** change spelling depending on their *mood*, *tense*, and *aspect*

# Word Order

- **descriptors** are placed *before* their target thing

| descriptor | ⬌ | thing |

- **definite articles** can appear as a *suffix* on its target, or as a separate word *before* its target thing if there is another descriptor associated with the target

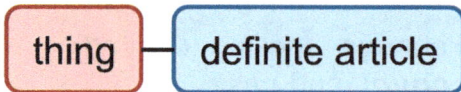

| thing | — | definite article |

| definite article | ⬌ | descriptor | ⬌ | thing |

- **indefinite article** is placed *before* its target thing

| indefinite article | ⬌ | thing |

- **thing-converters** are placed *before* the target thing and the target thing's descriptors

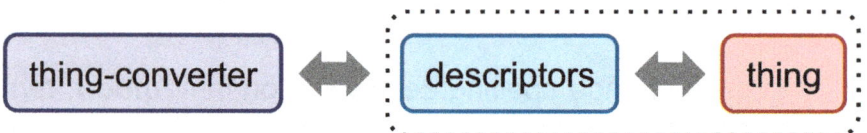

| thing-converter | ⬌ | descriptors | ⬌ | thing |

- there are four types of **scene**, and each type has a different complement of things; however, all four types have a thing that acts as the scene's verb, and a thing that acts as the scene's subject; in general, Danish scenes start with the subject, then the verb follows immediately afterwards

## linking

| subject | ⟷ | verb | ⟷ | thing / descriptor |

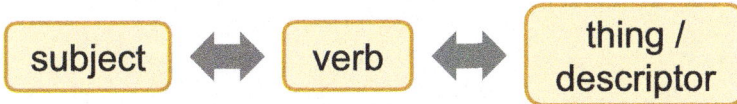

## intransitive

| subject | ⟷ | verb |

## monotransitive

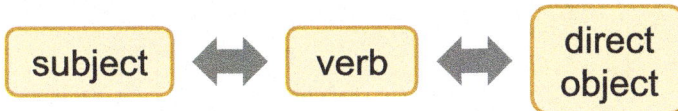

| subject | ⟷ | verb | ⟷ | direct object |

## ditransitive

| subject | ⟷ | verb | ⟷ | indirect object | ⟷ | direct object |

- **scene-converters** are placed *before* their target scene

| scene-converter | ⟷ | scene |

# Scenes

# What is a Scene

A scene is just a particular arrangement of things, where one of the things acts as a verb, and another as a subject.

The verb in a scene does not necessarily need to have a tense, it can be in an infinitive form or a continuous form.

Additionally, a scene can serve multiple purposes. It can serve as a complete sentence, standing on its own. It can also act as a thing or a descriptor, often with the help of a scene-converter word.

There are too many variations of scenes to show them all, but several will be demonstrated in this chapter.

The Danish version of the sentence 'She is happy' is:

| | | |
|---|---|---|
| **Hun er glad.** | | |
| hun | er | glad |
| she | is | happy |
| | **She is happy.** | |

The subject 'hun' is first, followed by the verb 'være' in one of its conjugated forms, and lastly the linking scene complement 'glad', which is a descriptor.

---

This is a graphical diagram of the sentence. The Danish words are in the middle, in solid yellow. The names of the components for this linking scene, i.e. subject, verb, and complement, are shown above, in black outline. The universal categories of each word are given below; things are red font, and descriptors are in blue font.

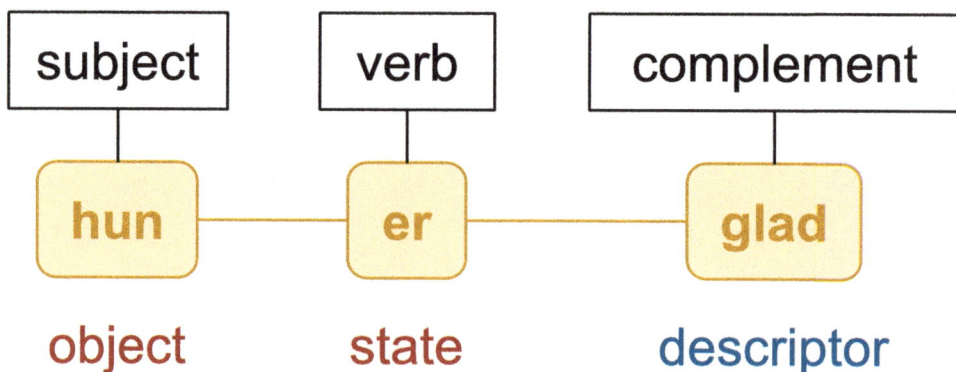

| subject | verb | complement |
|---|---|---|
| hun | er | glad |
| object | state | descriptor |

# Linking Scene as a Thing, with Tensed Verb

The Danish version of the sentence 'I know that she is happy' is:

| | | | | | | |
|---|---|---|---|---|---|---|
| **Jeg ved, at hun er glad.** | | | | | | |
| **jeg** | **ved** | **at** | **hun** | **er** | **glad** | |
| i | know | that | she | is | happy | |
| **I know that she is happy.** | | | | | | |

In this sentence, there are two scenes. One scene is the linking scene 'she is happy'. The other scene is 'I know [something]', which is a monotransitive scene. The linking scene is nested within the monotransitive scene.

Notice that the inner linking scene is preceded by the scene-converter word 'that', which helps to indicate that the linking scene is going to be used as a thing within an enclosing scene.

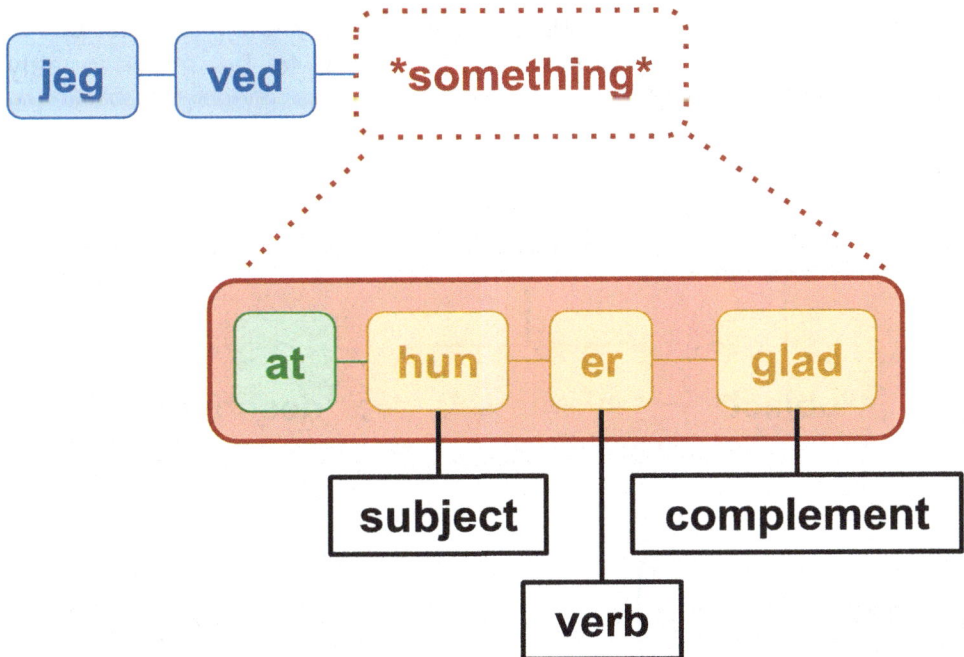

# Intransitive Scene as Sentence, Converted Thing as Descriptor

The Danish version of the sentence 'The man swam in the lake' is:

| | | | | | |
|---|---|---|---|---|---|
| **Manden svømmede i søen.** | | | | | |
| mand | -en | svømmede | i | sø | -en |
| man | the | swam | in | lake | the |
| **The man swam in the lake.** | | | | | |

The simplest version of this intransitive scene is 'The man swam'. However, the example sentence also has a thing-converter word, 'in', to convert an object, 'the lake', into a location. Hence the phrase 'in the lake' is called a converted thing. Here, the phrase 'in the lake' is acting as a descriptor of the process 'swam', which is the verb of the intransitive scene.

Note that even though the phrase 'in the lake' is used as a descriptor, it is placed at the very end of the sentence, instead of immediately in front of the verb it describes. This contradicts the general rule of Danish descriptors going before their targets, but in fact it is common for descriptors of verbs to be more loosely attached to their target.

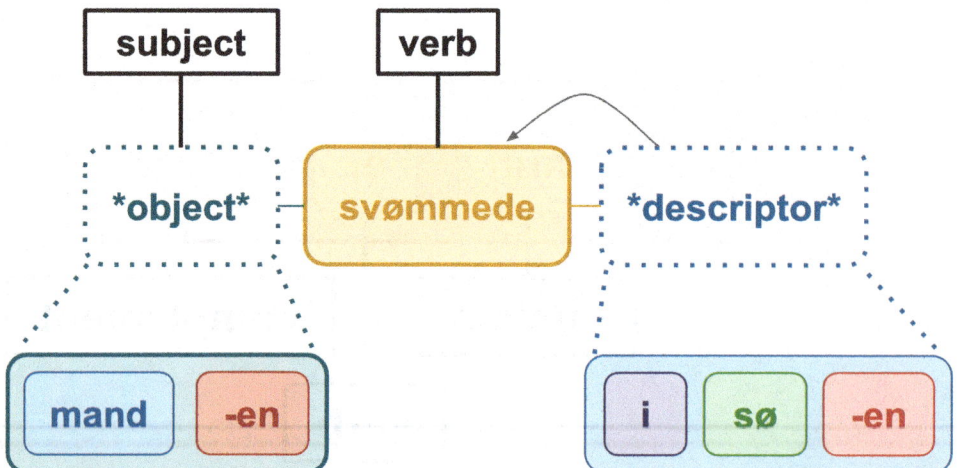

# Intransitive Scene as Thing, with Untensed Verb

The Danish version of the sentence 'I want them to sleep' is:

| Jeg vil, at de skal sove. | | | | | |
|---|---|---|---|---|---|
| jeg | vil | at | de | skal | sove |
| i | want | that | they | must | sleep |
| **I want them to sleep.** | | | | | |

The intransitive scene in this example is the nested 'they will sleep'.

The outer scene 'i want [something]' is a monotransitive scene.

The scene-converter word 'that' is used to help indicate the presence of a scene being used as an object.

---

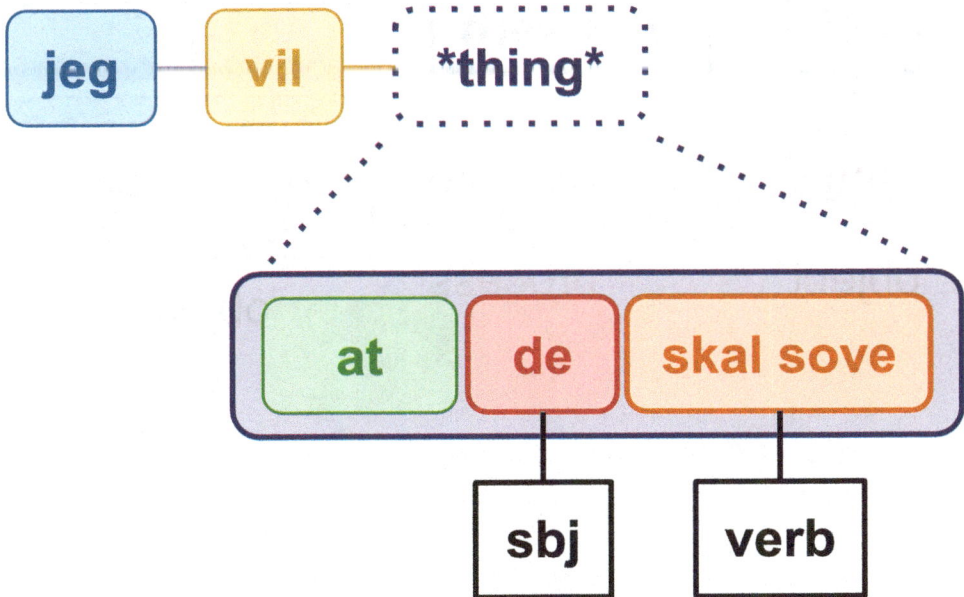

# Monotransitive Scene as Sentence

The Danish version of the sentence 'I will order a pizza' is:

| jeg | vil | bestille | en | pizza |
|-----|-----|----------|-----|-------|
| **Jeg vil bestille en pizza.** | | | | |
| i | will | order | a | pizza |
| **I will order a pizza.** | | | | |

In this example, the scene is a sentence. It is a monotransitive scene, so there is a verb, subject, and direct object. The verb is 'to order' in the future tense, and in both English and Danish the future tense is indicated by the addition of an auxiliary verb.

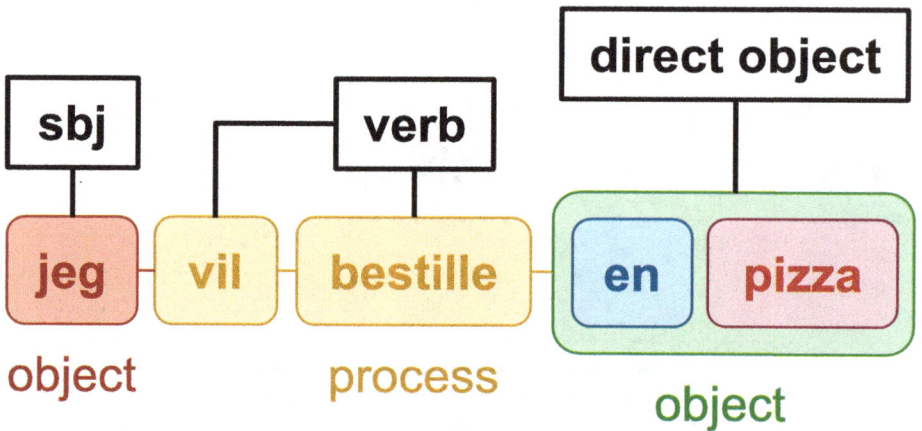

# Ditransitive Scene as Sentence

The Danish version of the sentence 'The girl passed her friend a note' is:

| | | | |
|---|---|---|---|
| **Pigen gav en besked til sin ven.** | | | |
| pig | -en | gav | en |
| girl | the | gave | a |
| besked | til | sin | ven |
| note | to | her | friend |
| **The girl passed her friend a note.** | | | |

However, notice that the Danish translation is not a ditransitive scene. Instead of an indirect object to indicate the recipient of the note, a converted thing (the prepositional phrase 'to her friend') is used instead to describe who got the note.

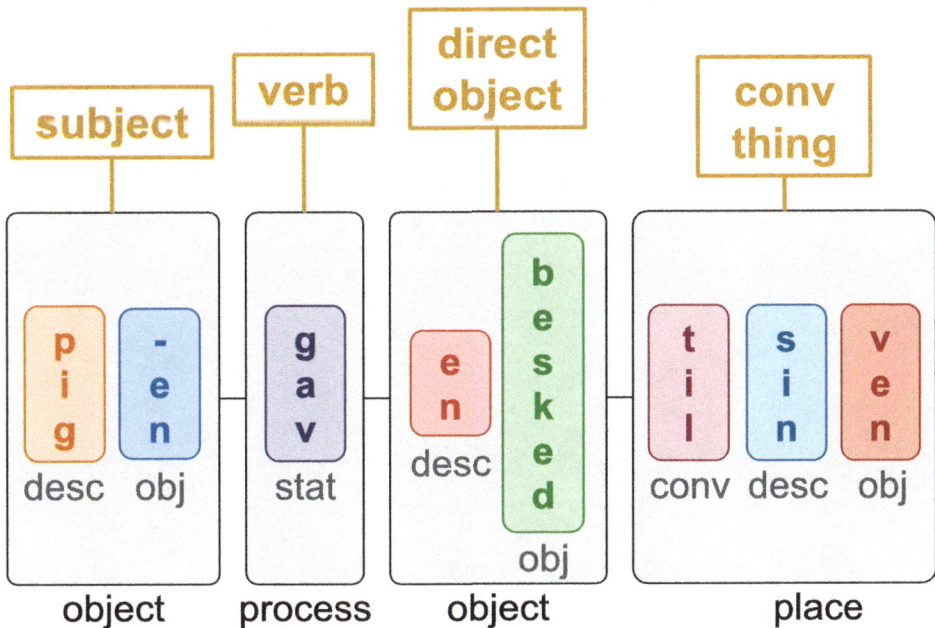

# Personal Pronouns

## as Subjects

| | |
|---|---|
| **jeg** | i |
| **vi** | we |
| **du** | you |
| **i** | you all |
| **han** | he |
| **hun** | she |
| **de** | they |

**Jeg** er en person.

| yai | er | een | persohn |
|-----|-----|-----|---------|
| jeg | er | en | person |
| i | am | a | person |

**I** am a person.

|        |           |          | case       |         |            |
|--------|-----------|----------|------------|---------|------------|
| persp  | gender    | count    | nominative | oblique | possessive |
| 1st    | any       | singular | **jeg**    | mig     | min mit mine |
|        |           | plural   | vi         | os      | vores      |
| 2nd    | any       | singular | du         | dig     | din dit dine |
|        |           | plural   | i          | jer     | jeres      |
| 3rd    | masculine | singular | han        | ham     | hans       |
|        | feminine  | singular | hun        | hende   | hendes     |
|        | common    | singular | den        | den     | dens       |
|        | neuter    | singular | det        | det     | dets       |
|        | any       | plural   | de         | dem     | deres      |

# Pigerne, **de** er glade.

| peega | ne | 3rd person, plural, feminine, nominative<br>dee | ehr | glaid |
|-------|-----|-----|-----|-------|
| piger | -ne | **de** | er | glade |
| girls | the | they | are | glad |

## The girls, **they** are happy.

| persp | gender | count | nominative | oblique | possessive |
|-------|--------|-------|------------|---------|------------|
| | | | | case | |
| 1st | any | singular | jeg | mig | min mit mine |
| | | plural | vi | os | vores |
| 2nd | any | singular | du | dig | din dit dine |
| | | plural | i | jer | jeres |
| 3rd | masculine | singular | han | ham | hans |
| | feminine | singular | hun | hende | hendes |
| | common | singular | den | den | dens |
| | neuter | singular | det | det | dets |
| | any | plural | **de** | dem | deres |

**Vi** så en film.

| vee | soh | een | film |
| vi | så | en | film |
| we | saw | a | film |

**We** watched a movie.

| | | | | case | |
| persp | gender | count | nominative | oblique | possessive |
| 1st | any | singular | jeg | mig | min mit mine |
| | | plural | **vi** | os | vores |
| 2nd | any | singular | du | dig | din dit dine |
| | | plural | i | jer | jeres |
| 3rd | masculine | singular | han | ham | hans |
| | feminine | singular | hun | hende | hendes |
| | common | singular | den | den | dens |
| | neuter | singular | det | det | dets |
| | any | plural | de | dem | deres |

**Du** taler.

tayleh
taler
talk

**You** are talking.

| persp | gender | count | nominative | case oblique | possessive |
|-------|--------|-------|------------|--------------|------------|
| 1st | any | singular | jeg | mig | min mit mine |
| | | plural | vi | os | vores |
| 2nd | any | singular | **du** | dig | din dit dine |
| | | plural | i | jer | jeres |
| 3rd | masculine | singular | han | ham | hans |
| | feminine | singular | hun | hende | hendes |
| | common | singular | den | den | dens |
| | neuter | singular | det | det | dets |
| | any | plural | de | dem | deres |

# Personal Pronouns
## as Direct Objects

| | |
|---|---|
| **mig** | me |
| **os** | us |
| **dig** | you |
| **jer** | you all |
| **ham** | him |
| **hende** | her |
| **dem** | them |

# Jeg kan se **dig**.

| | | | |
|---|---|---|---|
| yai | kan | see | dai |
| jeg | kan | se | dig |
| i | can | see | you |

## I see **you**.

| persp | gender | count | case nominative | oblique | possessive |
|---|---|---|---|---|---|
| 1st | any | singular | jeg | mig | min mit mine |
| | | plural | vi | os | vores |
| 2nd | any | singular | du | **dig** | din dit dine |
| | | plural | i | jer | jeres |
| 3rd | masculine | singular | han | ham | hans |
| | feminine | singular | hun | hende | hendes |
| | common | singular | den | den | dens |
| | neuter | singular | det | det | dets |
| | any | plural | de | dem | deres |

# Du satte **mig** i båden.

| du | satteh | mai | ee | boa | en |
|----|--------|-----|-----|-----|-----|
| du | satte | **mig** | i | båd | -en |
| you | put | me | in | boat | the |

## You put **me** in the boat.

| | | | case | | |
|---|---|---|---|---|---|
| persp | gender | count | nominative | oblique | possessive |
| 1st | any | singular | jeg | **mig** | min mit mine |
| | | plural | vi | os | vores |
| 2nd | any | singular | du | dig | din dit dine |
| | | plural | i | jer | jeres |
| 3rd | masculine | singular | han | ham | hans |
| | feminine | singular | hun | hende | hendes |
| | common | singular | den | den | dens |
| | neuter | singular | det | det | dets |
| | any | plural | de | dem | deres |

# De kører **os** til biblioteket.

| dee | kuhreh | 1st person, plural, oblique os | til | bibliotek | et |
|-----|--------|------|-----|-----------|-----|
| de | kører | os | til | bibliotek | -et |
| they | drives | us | to | library | the |

# They take **us** to the library.

| persp | gender | count | nominative | case oblique | possessive |
|-------|--------|-------|------------|--------------|------------|
| 1st | any | singular | jeg | mig | min mit mine |
| | | plural | vi | os | vores |
| 2nd | any | singular | du | dig | din dit dine |
| | | plural | i | jer | jeres |
| 3rd | masculine | singular | han | ham | hans |
| | feminine | singular | hun | hende | hendes |
| | common | singular | den | den | dens |
| | neuter | singular | det | det | dets |
| | any | plural | de | dem | deres |

# Vi skubber **dem** i floden.

| vee | skobeh | 3rd person, plural, oblique<br>dem | ee | flod | en |
|-----|--------|------|-----|------|-----|
| vi | skubber | dem | i | flod | -en |
| we | push | them | in | river | the |

## We push **them** into the river.

| persp | gender | count | nominative | oblique | possessive |
|-------|--------|-------|------------|---------|------------|
| | | | | case | |
| 1st | any | singular | jeg | mig | min mit mine |
| | | plural | vi | os | vores |
| 2nd | any | singular | du | dig | din dit dine |
| | | plural | i | jer | jeres |
| 3rd | masculine | singular | han | ham | hans |
| | feminine | singular | hun | hende | hendes |
| | common | singular | den | den | dens |
| | neuter | singular | det | det | dets |
| | any | plural | de | **dem** | deres |

# Personal Pronouns

## as Indirect Objects

| | |
|---|---|
| **mig** | me |
| **os** | us |
| **dig** | you |
| **jer** | you all |
| **ham** | him |
| **hende** | her |
| **dem** | them |

# Du giver **mig** en bog.

| doo | geeveh | 1st person, singular, oblique<br>mai | een | bok |
|-----|--------|------|-----|-----|
| du | giver | **mig** | en | bog |
| you | give | **me** | a | book |

## You give **me** a book.

|  |  |  |  | case |  |
|------|--------|----------|------------|---------|-------------|
| persp | gender | count | nominative | oblique | possessive |
| 1st | any | singular | jeg | **mig** | min mit mine |
|  |  | plural | vi | os | vores |
| 2nd | any | singular | du | dig | din dit dine |
|  |  | plural | i | jer | jeres |
| 3rd | masculine | singular | han | ham | hans |
|  | feminine | singular | hun | hende | hendes |
|  | common | singular | den | den | dens |
|  | neuter | singular | det | det | dets |
|  | any | plural | de | dem | deres |

# Han kaster **hende** bolden.

| hahn | kasteh | **3rd person, singular, feminine, oblique** hayn-eh | boll | en |
|------|--------|----------------------------------------------------|------|-----|
| han | kaster | **hende** | bold | -en |
| he | throws | her | ball | the |

# He throws **her** the ball.

| persp | gender | count | nominative | case oblique | possessive |
|-------|--------|-------|------------|--------------|------------|
| 1st | any | singular | jeg | mig | min mit mine |
|     |     | plural | vi | os | vores |
| 2nd | any | singular | du | dig | din dit dine |
|     |     | plural | i | jer | jeres |
| 3rd | masculine | singular | han | ham | hans |
|     | feminine | singular | hun | **hende** | hendes |
|     | common | singular | den | den | dens |
|     | neuter | singular | det | det | dets |
|     | any | plural | de | dem | deres |

# Vi viser **dem** et billede.

| vee | veeseh | 3rd person, plural, oblique<br>**dem** | et | beel-eh |
|-----|--------|------|-----|---------|
| vi | viser | **dem** | et | billede |
| we | show | **them** | a | painting |

## We show **them** a painting.

| persp | gender | count | nominative | case<br>oblique | possessive |
|-------|--------|-------|------------|--------|------------|
| 1st | any | singular | jeg | mig | min mit mine |
| | | plural | vi | os | vores |
| 2nd | any | singular | du | dig | din dit dine |
| | | plural | i | jer | jeres |
| 3rd | masculine | singular | han | ham | hans |
| | feminine | singular | hun | hende | hendes |
| | common | singular | den | den | dens |
| | neuter | singular | det | det | dets |
| | any | plural | de | **dem** | deres |

37

## Jeg giver **dig** pizzaen.

| yai | geeveh | 2nd person, singular, oblique<br>dai | pizza | en |
|-----|--------|------|-------|-----|
| jeg | giver | dig | pizza | -en |
| i | give | you | pizza | the |

## I give **you** the pizza.

|  |  |  | | case | |
|------|----------|----------|------------|---------|----------------|
| persp | gender | count | nominative | oblique | possessive |
| 1st | any | singular | jeg | mig | min mit mine |
|  |  | plural | vi | os | vores |
| 2nd | any | singular | du | **dig** | din dit dine |
|  |  | plural | i | jer | jeres |
| 3rd | masculine | singular | han | ham | hans |
|  | feminine | singular | hun | hende | hendes |
|  | common | singular | den | den | dens |
|  | neuter | singular | det | det | dets |
|  | any | plural | de | dem | deres |

# Things

Things have
- gender [ **common** / **neuter** ]
- count [ **single** / **plural** ]

and they can change spelling for count, usually by adding **-e** or **-r**, as well as depending on which article is used, definite or indefinite.

Definite article is added as a suffix to its target thing [ **-en** / **-et** / **-ne** ], except when there is an adjective, and then the definite article changes to [ **den** / **det** / **de** ] and goes in front of the target. It changes spelling to match the target's gender and count.

Indefinite article always goes in front of its target thing [ **en** / **et** ]. It changes spelling to match the target's gender.

|  |  |  | *common* |
|---|---|---|---|
|  | boy |  | dreng |
|  | boys |  | dreng**e** |
| **the** | boy |  | dreng**en** |
| **the** | boys |  | dreng**ene** |
| **a** | boy | **en** | dreng |
| **some** | boys | **nogle** | dreng**e** |
|  | short boy |  | kort dreng |
|  | short boys |  | korte dreng**e** |
| **the** | short boy | **den** | korte dreng |
| **the** | short boys | **de** | korte dreng**e** |
| **a** | short boy | **en** | kort dreng |
| **some** | short boys | **nogle** | korte dreng**e** |

40

|  | English |  | *neuter* |
|---|---|---|---|
|  | house |  | hus |
|  | houses |  | huse |
| the | house |  | huset |
| the | houses |  | husene |
| a | house | et | hus |
| some | houses | nogle | huse |

|  | English |  | *neuter* |
|---|---|---|---|
|  | big house |  | stort hus |
|  | big houses |  | store huse |
| the | big house | det | store hus |
| the | big houses | de | store huse |
| a | big house | et | stort hus |
| some | big houses | nogle | store huse |

## Han spiste et **æble**.

| | | INDEFINITE ARTICLE | neuter, singular |
|---|---|---|---|
| han | speeste | et | eble |
| han | spiste | et | æble |
| he | ate | an | apple |

## He ate an **apple**.

### Apple / Æble

neuter

|  | singular | plural |
|---|---|---|
| indefinite | **æble** | æbler |
| definite | æblet | æblerne |

# De fandt et grønt **æble**.

| deh | fand | INDEFINITE ARTICLE et | gront | neuter, singular eble |
|-----|------|-----|-------|----------------|
| de | fandt | et | grønt | **æble** |
| they | found | a | green | apple |

## They found a green **apple**.

### Apple / Æble

neuter

| | singular | plural |
|---|---|---|
| indefinite | **æble** | æbler |
| definite | æblet | æblerne |

# **Mand**en synger.

| common, singular | DEFINITE ARTICLE | |
|---|---|---|
| mand | en | singer |
| mand | -en | synger |
| man | the | sings |

## The **man** is singing.

### Man / Mand

common

| | singular | plural |
|---|---|---|
| indefinite | **mand** | mænd |
| definite | manden | mændene |

42

# Den gamle **mand** drikker te.

| DEFINITE ARTICLE | | common, singular | | |
|---|---|---|---|---|
| den | gamla | mand | drikker | tee |
| den | gamle | mand | drikker | te |
| the | old | man | drinks | tea |

## The old **man** is drinking tea.

### Man / Mand

common

| | singular | plural |
|---|---|---|
| indefinite | **mand** | mænd |
| definite | manden | mændene |

# Hun kastede **æble**t.

| | | neuter, singular | DEFINITE ARTICLE |
|---|---|---|---|
| hoon | kastede | eble | et |
| hun | kastede | æble | -et |
| she | cast | apple | the |

## She threw the **apple**.

### Apple / Æble

neuter

| | singular | plural |
|---|---|---|
| indefinite | **æble** | æbler |
| definite | æblet | æblerne |

# Det gamle **æble** er blødt.

| DEFINITE ARTICLE | | neuter, singular | | |
|---|---|---|---|---|
| det | gamla | eble | ehr | blod |
| det | gamle | **æble** | er | **blødt** |
| the | old | apple | is | soft |

## The old **apple** is soft.

### Apple / Æble

| neuter | | |
|---|---|---|
| | singular | plural |
| indefinite | **æble** | æbler |
| definite | æblet | æblerne |

# De fandt de unge **mænd**.

| | | DEFINITE ARTICLE | | common, plural |
|---|---|---|---|---|
| dee | fahnd | dee | ung | mand |
| de | fandt | de | unge | **mænd** |
| they | found | the | young | men |

## The found the young **men**.

### Man / Mand

| common | | |
|---|---|---|
| | singular | plural |
| indefinite | mand | **mænd** |
| definite | manden | mændene |

# Æblerne er i skålen.

| neuter, plural | DEFINITE ARTICLE | | | | |
|---|---|---|---|---|---|
| ebler | ne | ehr | ee | skal | en |
| æbler | -ne | er | i | skål | -en |
| apples | the | are | in | bowl | the |

## The **apples** are in the bowl.

### Apple / Æble

neuter

| | singular | plural |
|---|---|---|
| indefinite | æble | **æbler** |
| definite | æblet | æblerne |

# Vi tog de røde **æbler** med.

| | | DEFINITE ARTICLE | | neuter, plural | |
|---|---|---|---|---|---|
| vee | tok | deh | rod | ebler | med |
| vi | tog | de | røde | æbler | med |
| we | took | the | red | apples | with |

## We brought the red **apples**.

### Apple / Æble

neuter

| | singular | plural |
|---|---|---|
| indefinite | æble | **æbler** |
| definite | æblet | æblerne |

# Definite Article

## Target Thing's

| +Adj | Gender | Count | | | | |
|------|--------|-------|-----|-----|-------|-----|
| no | common | singular | | | thing | **en** |
| no | neuter | singular | | | thing | **et** |
| no | either | plural | | | thing | **ne** |
| yes | common | singular | **den** | adj | thing | |
| yes | neuter | singular | **det** | adj | thing | |
| yes | either | plural | **de** | adj | thing | |

## Jeg ser pigen.

| | | common, singular | common, ← singular |
|------|------|------------------|--------------------|
| yai | ser | peeg | en |
| jeg | ser | pige | -en |
| i | see | girl | the |

## I see **the** girl.

| matches target's: | | + descriptor | |
|-------------------|----------|-----|-----|
| *gender* | *count* | yes | no |
| common | singular | den | **-en** |
| neuter | singular | det | -et |
| either | plural | de | -ne |

# Den lille bil er hurtig.

| common, singular → | *attributive descriptor* | common, singular | | |
|---|---|---|---|---|
| den | leel | beel | ehr | hoortihg |
| den | lille | bil | er | hurtig |
| the | little | car | is | fast |

## The small car is fast.

| matches target's: | | + descriptor | |
|---|---|---|---|
| *gender* | *count* | yes | no |
| common | singular | **den** | -en |
| neuter | singular | det | -et |
| either | plural | de | -ne |

# Huset er dit.

| neuter, singular | ← neuter, singular | | |
|---|---|---|---|
| hoos | et | ehr | deet |
| hus | -et | er | dit |
| house | the | is | yours |

## The house is yours.

| matches target's: | | + descriptor | |
|---|---|---|---|
| *gender* | *count* | yes | no |
| common | singular | den | -en |
| neuter | singular | det | **-et** |
| either | plural | de | -ne |

# Drenge**ne** spiser frokost.

| common, plural | common, ← plural | | |
|---|---|---|---|
| drengeh | neh | speeseh | frhokost |
| drenge | -ne | spiser | frokost |
| boys | the | eat | lunch |

## **The** boys eat lunch.

| matches target's | | + descriptor | |
|---|---|---|---|
| gender | count | yes | no |
| common | singular | den | -en |
| neuter | singular | det | -et |
| either | plural | de | **-ne** |

# **De** røde huse er nye.

| neuter, plural → | *attributive descriptor* | neuter, plural | | |
|---|---|---|---|---|
| dee | rhood | hooseh | ehr | new |
| de | røde | huse | er | nye |
| the | red | houses | are | new |

## **The** red houses are new.

| matches target's: | | + descriptor | |
|---|---|---|---|
| gender | count | yes | no |
| common | singular | den | -en |
| neuter | singular | det | -et |
| either | plural | **de** | -ne |

# Indefinite Article

| +Adj | Target Thing's Gender | Count | | | |
|------|--------|----------|-----|-----|-------|
| no   | common | singular | **en** | | thing |
| no   | neuter | singular | **et** | | thing |
| yes  | common | singular | **en** | adj | thing |
| yes  | neuter | singular | **et** | adj | thing |

## Jeg spiser **et** æble.

| | | neuter, singular → | neuter, singular |
|---|---|---|---|
| yai | speeseh | et | aybleh |
| jeg | spiser | et | æble |
| i | eat | an | apple |

## I eat **an** apple.

*matches target's:*

| gender | count | |
|--------|----------|-----|
| common | singular | en |
| neuter | singular | **et** |

# En kvinde styrer båden.

| common, singular → | common, singular | | | |
|---|---|---|---|---|
| een | kveeneh | stureh | boat | en |
| en | kvinde | styrer | båd | -en |
| a | woman | drives | boat | the |

## A woman is driving the boat.

*matches target's:*

| *gender* | *count* | |
|---|---|---|
| common | singular | **en** |
| neuter | singular | et |

# En grøn fugl ser en orm.

| common, singular → | common, singular | | | |
|---|---|---|---|---|
| een | groyn | fooghel | ser | een | orm |
| en | grøn | fugl | ser | en | orm |
| a | green | bird | sees | a | worm |

## A green bird sees a worm.

*matches target's:*

| *gender* | *count* | |
|---|---|---|
| common | singular | **en** |
| neuter | singular | et |

# Han har **en** bluse på.

| | | common,<br>singular → | common,<br>singular | |
|---|---|---|---|---|
| han | hahr | een | blooseh | poh |
| han | har | en | bluse | på |
| he | has | a | shirt | on |

# He is wearing **a** shirt.

*matches target's:*

| gender | count | |
|---|---|---|
| common | singular | **en** |
| neuter | singular | et |

# De sover på **et** hotel.

| | | | neuter,<br>singular → | neuter,<br>singular |
|---|---|---|---|---|
| dee | soh-ur | poh | et | hotel |
| de | sover | på | et | hotel |
| they | sleep | in | a | hotel |

# They sleep in **a** hotel.

*matches target's:*

| gender | count | |
|---|---|---|
| common | singular | en |
| neuter | singular | **et** |

# Descriptors for

## objects
## concepts
## times
## places

## As a Linking Scene Complement

When a descriptor is used in the complement slot of a linking scene, it matches the gender and count of the scene's subject.

## As an Immediate Attribute to a Thing

When not placed in the complement position of a linking scene, descriptors are used as immediate neighbors to things. When used in this manner, they go before their target, and they change spelling to match their target thing's gender and count, as well as depending on which article is used, definite or indefinite.

# Det **store** hus er på bakken.

| DEFINITE ARTICLE | *attributive descriptor* [neuter, singular] → | neuter, singular | | | | |
|---|---|---|---|---|---|---|
| deh | sto-eh | hoos | ehr | poh | bakke | n |
| det | store | hus | er | på | bakke | -n |
| the | big | house | is | on | hill | the |

# The **big** house is on the hill.

## Big / Stor

*attributive (and predicative) forms:*

| noun → | common singular | common plural | neuter singular | neuter plural |
|---|---|---|---|---|
| - definite article | stor | store | stort | store |
| + definite article | store | store | **store** | store |

# Jeg købte en **ny** hat.

| | | INDEFINITE ARTICLE | *attributive descriptor* matches [common, singular] noun → | common, singular |
|---|---|---|---|---|
| yai | kobt | en | ny | haht |
| jeg | købte | en | ny | hat |
| i | bought | a | new | hat |

# I bought a **new** hat.

## New / Ny

*attributive (and predicative) forms:*

| noun → | common singular | common plural | neuter singular | neuter plural |
|---|---|---|---|---|
| - definite article | **ny** | nye | nyt | nye |
| + definite article | nye | nye | nye | nye |

# Det er **godt**.

| 3rd person, singular, neuter | | *predicative descriptor* matches ← [neuter, singular] subject |
|---|---|---|
| det | ehr | goht |
| det | er | godt |
| it | is | good |

## It is **good**.

### Good / God

*attributive (and predicative) forms:*

| noun → | common singular | common plural | neuter singular | neuter plural |
|---|---|---|---|---|
| - definite article | god | gode | **godt** | gode |
| + definite article | gode | gode | gode | gode |

# Vi lytter til **høj** musik.

| | | | *attributive descriptor* matches [common, singular] noun → | common, singular |
|---|---|---|---|---|
| vee | lutteh | til | hoi | moosic |
| vi | lytter | til | høj | musik |
| we | listen | to | loud | music |

## We listen to **loud** music.

### Loud / Høj

*attributive (and predicative) forms:*

| noun → | common singular | common plural | neuter singular | neuter plural |
|---|---|---|---|---|
| - definite article | **høj** | høje | højt | høje |
| + definite article | høje | høje | høje | høje |

# Jeg købte et **stort** hus.

| | | INDEFINITE ARTICLE | *attributive descriptor* matches [neuter, singular] noun → | neuter, singular |
|---|---|---|---|---|
| yai | koobteh | eh | stoh | hoos |
| jeg | købte | et | **stort** | hus |
| i | bought | a | big | house |

# I bought a **big** house.

### Big / Stor

*attributive (and predicative) forms:*

| noun → | common singular | common plural | neuter singular | neuter plural |
|---|---|---|---|---|
| - definite article | stor | store | **stort** | store |
| + definite article | store | store | store | store |

# Den **høje** musik kommer fra radioen.

| DEFINITE ARTICLE | *attributive descriptor* [common, singular]→ | common, singular | | | | |
|---|---|---|---|---|---|---|
| den | hoya | musik | kommeh | fra | rahdio | en |
| den | høje | musik | kommer | fra | radio | -en |
| the | loud | music | comes | from | radio | the |

# The **loud** music is coming from the radio.

### Loud / Høj

*attributive (and predicative) forms:*

| noun → | common singular | common plural | neuter singular | neuter plural |
|---|---|---|---|---|
| - definite article | høj | høje | højt | høje |
| + definite article | **høje** | høje | høje | høje |

# Han fangede en **lille** fisk.

| | | INDEFINITE ARTICLE | *attributive descriptor* matches [common, singular] noun → | common, singular |
|---|---|---|---|---|
| hahn | fangede | en | lil | fisk |
| han | fangede | en | lille | fisk |
| he | caught | a | little | fish |

# He caught a **small** fish.

## Small / Lille

*attributive (and predicative) forms:*

| noun → | common singular | common plural | neuter singular | neuter plural |
|---|---|---|---|---|
| - definite article | **lille** | små | lille | små |
| + definite article | små | små | små | små |

# Voksne er **gamle**.

| common, plural | | *predicative descriptor* ← matches [common, plural] noun |
|---|---|---|
| voksna | ehr | gamle |
| voksne | er | gamle |
| adults | are | old |

# Adults are **old**.

## New / Ny

*attributive (and predicative) forms:*

| noun → | common singular | common plural | neuter singular | neuter plural |
|---|---|---|---|---|
| - definite article | gammel | **gamle** | gammelt | gamle |
| + definite article | gamle | gamle | gamle | gamle |

# Descriptors for

## processes
## states

## Not Used as a Linking Scene Complement

Descriptors for processes or states are usually not used as the complement item of a linking scene.

## As an Immediate Attribute

It is much more common to use descriptors of processes and states in the attributive manner, regardless of whether or not their target is being used as the verb in a scene or as a thing.

Hun løber **hurtigt**.

| | thing | descriptor |
|---|---|---|
| hoon | loopeh | huhr-teeg |
| hun | løber | hurtigt |
| she | runs | quickly |

She runs **quickly**.


Han er **altid** sulten.

| | thing | descriptor | |
|---|---|---|---|
| hahn | ehr | altid | sulten |
| han | er | altid | sulten |
| he | is | always | hungry |

He is **always** hungry.


Vi synger **lykkeligt**.

| | thing | descriptor |
|---|---|---|
| vee | sing-eh | leh-ke-leed |
| vi | synger | lykkeligt |
| we | sing | happily |

We sing **happily**.

# Descriptor + Thing

## Example Sentences

**Den lille kat** hopper.

| common, singular → | common, singular → | common, singular | |
|---|---|---|---|
| den | leel | kat | hoppeh |
| den | lille | kat | hopper |
| the | little | cat | jumps |

**The small cat** jumps.

**Den høje, tynde mand** drikker.

| common, singular → | common, singular → | common, singular → | common, singular | |
|---|---|---|---|---|
| den | hoi | tinneh | man | dreykeh |
| den | høje | tynde | mand | drikker |
| the | tall | thin | man | drinks |

**The tall, thin man** drinks.

**Den brune ko** sover.

| common, singular → | common, singular → | common, singular | |
|---|---|---|---|
| den | bruneh | koh | soh-ehr |
| den | brune | ko | sover |
| the | brown | cow | sleeps |

**The brown cow** sleeps.

## Han ser **en klog kvinde**.

| han | ser | common, singular → | common, singular → | common, singular |
|---|---|---|---|---|
| | | een | kloh | kveen |
| han | ser | en | klog | kvinde |
| he | sees | a | smart | woman |

He sees **a smart woman**.

## **Mine fire orange fisk** svømmer.

| common, plural → | → | common, plural → | common, plural | |
|---|---|---|---|---|
| meeneh | feer | oranjeh | fisk | svemmeh |
| mine | fire | orange | fisk | svømmer |
| my | 4 | orange | fish | swim |

**My four orange fish** swim.

## **Deres køkken** har **mange store vinduer**.

| neuter, singular → | neuter, singular | hah | neuter, plural → | neuter, plural → | neuter, plural |
|---|---|---|---|---|---|
| deh-ehs | kooken | hah | mangeh | sto-eh | vindueh |
| deres | køkken | har | mange | store | vinduer |
| their | kitchen | has | many | big | windows |

**Their kitchen** has **many big windows**.

## Der er **fire små, røde fugle** her.

| der | ehr | → feer | common, plural → smoh | common, plural → royd | common, plural fooleh | hee-yeh |
|-----|-----|--------|------------------------|------------------------|------------------------|---------|
| der | er | fire | små | røde | fugle | her |
| there | are | 4 | small | red | birds | here |

## There are **four small, red birds** here.

## Jeg vil spise **ti søde småkager**.

| yai | veel gern | speese | → tee | common, plural → soode | common, plural smoh-kay-eh |
|-----|-----------|--------|-------|-------------------------|-----------------------------|
| jeg | vil gerne | spise | ti | søde | småkager |
| i | want | eat | 10 | sweet | cookies |

## I want to eat **ten sweet cookies**.

## **Fjorten brune orme** bor under jorden

| → fyor-en | common, plural → bruhn | common, plural ormeh | bohr | un-ehr | yor-en |
|-----------|-------------------------|-----------------------|------|--------|--------|
| fjorten | brune | orme | bor | under | jorden |
| 14 | brown | worms | live | under | ground |

## **Fourteen brown worms** live underground.

# Verbs

# What are Verbs

Verbs are processes or states that are used in the verb slot of a scene. In Danish, verbs have mood, tense, and aspect. *Also, it should be noted that, unlike English verbs, Danish verbs do not change spelling to match their scene's subject.*

## 1 - Moods

There are three moods in Danish: indicative, subjunctive, and imperative.

- *Imperative* is used for giving commands.
- *Subjunctive* is to express a personal belief or opinion.
- *Indicative* is for making statements of facts or talking about things that are known as being true.

In this book, only the indicative is discussed, as it is the most commonly used mood.

## 2 - Tense

There are three tenses in Danish: *past*, *present*, and *future*. These are self explanatory. Past tense is used to discuss things in the past, present tense for the present, and future tense for things that will happen in the future.

## 3 - Aspect

There are two aspects: *imperfect / continuous* and *perfect*.

- *Imperfect* refers to processes or states that do not have a clear ending point, or have not ended yet.
- *Perfect* refers to processes or states that do have a clear ending point, or have already finished.

## Spelling and Extra Words

Danish verbs recognize these three characteristics, either by adding so-called auxiliary verbs or by changing their spelling. Examples of this are demonstrated in the remainder of this chapter.

Danish verbs do not change spelling to match the subject…

| | | |
|---|---|---|
| jeg **spiser** | i **eat** | |
| vi **spiser** | we **eat** | |
| du **spiser** | you **eat** | |
| i **spiser** | you all **eat** | |
| han **spiser** | he **eats** | |
| hun **spiser** | she **eats** | |
| de **spiser** | they **eat** | |

but they do change spelling for tense and aspect.

| jeg | | **spiste** | i | | | **ate** |
|---|---|---|---|---|---|---|
| jeg | | **spiste** | i | | was | **eating** |
| jeg | havde | **spist** | i | had | | **eaten** |
| jeg | havde | **spist** | i | had | been | **eating** |
| | | | | | | |
| jeg | | **spiser** | i | | | **eat** |
| jeg | | **spiser** | i | | am | **eating** |
| jeg | har | **spist** | i | have | | **eaten** |
| jeg | har | **spist** | i | have | been | **eating** |
| | | | | | | |
| jeg | vil | **spise** | i | will | | **eat** |
| jeg | vil | **spise** | i | will | be | **eating** |
| jeg | vil have | **spist** | i | will have | | **eaten** |
| jeg | vil have | **spist** | i | will have | been | **eating** |

# Jeg **gik** hen til butikken.

| yai | past<br>gik | hen | till | buteek | en |
|-----|-----|-----|------|--------|-----|
| jeg | gik | hen | til | butik | -en |
| i | went | to | to | store | the |

## I **went** to the store.

### To Go / Gå

**indicative mood:**

| tense | aspect | |
|-------|--------|--|
| | imperfect | perfect |
| past | **gik** | var gået |
| present | går | er gået |
| future | vil gå | vil være gået |

# De **fløj**.

| deh | past<br>floy |
|-----|------|
| de | fløj |
| they | flew |

## They **were flying**.

### To Fly / Flyve

**indicative mood:**

| tense | aspect | |
|-------|--------|--|
| | imperfect | perfect |
| past | **fløj** | var fløjet |
| present | flyver | er fløjet |
| future | vil flyve | vil være fløjet |

## Jeg **talte** i går.

| yai | past<br>talte | i gor |
|-----|------|-------|
| jeg | talte | i går |
| i | talked | yesterday |

## I **had spoken** yesterday.

### To Talk / Tale

indicative mood:

| | aspect | |
|--------|-----------|-----------|
| **tense** | imperfect | perfect |
| past | **talte** | havde talt |
| present | taler | har talt |
| future | vil tale | vil have talt |


## Hun **svømmede** inden da.

| hoon | past<br>svommede | inden | da |
|------|---------|-------|-----|
| hun | svømmede | inden | da |
| she | swam | before | when |

## She **had been swimming** before then.

### To Swim / Svømme

indicative mood:

| | aspect | |
|--------|-----------|-----------|
| **tense** | imperfect | perfect |
| past | **svømmede** | havde svømmet |
| present | svømmer | har svømmet |
| future | vil svømme | vil have svømmet |

Vi **har** fem hunde.

| vee | present<br>hahr | fem | hoonde |
|-----|------|-----|--------|
| vi | har | fem | hunde |
| we | have | 5 | dogs |

We **have** five dogs.

## To Have / Have

**indicative mood:**

| tense | aspect<br>imperfect | perfect |
|-------|-----------|---------|
| past | havde | havde haft |
| present | **har** | har haft |
| future | vil have | vil have haft |

Du **hopper**.

| doo | present<br>hoppar |
|-----|------|
| du | hopper |
| you | hop |

You **are jumping**.

## To Jump / Hoppe

**indicative mood:**

| tense | aspect<br>imperfect | perfect |
|-------|-----------|---------|
| past | hoppede | havde hoppet |
| present | **hopper** | har hoppet |
| future | vil hoppe | vil have hoppet |

## Du **har spurgt** mange gange.

| | present | past participle | | |
|---|---|---|---|---|
| doo | har | sporht | mange | gange |
| du | har | spurgt | mange | gange |
| you | have | asked | many | times |

## You **have asked** many times.

### To Ask / Spørge

indicative mood:

| tense | aspect | |
|---|---|---|
| | imperfect | perfect |
| past | spurgte | havde spurgt |
| present | spørger | **har spurgt** |
| future | vil spørge | vil have spurgt |


## Vi **har spillet** computerspil i dag.

| | present | past participle | | |
|---|---|---|---|---|
| vcc | hahr | spcclct | computcr spccl | cc dag |
| vi | har | spillet | computerspil | i dag |
| we | have | played | computer game | today |

## Today, we **have been playing** computer.

### To Play / Spille

indicative mood:

| tense | aspect | |
|---|---|---|
| | imperfect | perfect |
| past | spillede | havde spillet |
| present | spiller | **har spillet** |
| future | vil spille | vil have spillet |

# I morgen **skriver** hun en historie.

| | present | | | |
|---|---|---|---|---|
| ee morgen | skreeve | hoon | en | historie |
| i morgen | skriver | hun | en | historie |
| tomorrow | writes | she | a | history |

## Tomorrow, she **will write** a story.

### To Write / Skrive

**indicative mood:**

| | aspect | |
|---|---|---|
| **tense** | imperfect | perfect |
| past | skrev | havde skrevet |
| present | **skriver** | har skrevet |
| future | vil skrive | vil have skrevet |

# De **vil studere**.

| | present | infinitive |
|---|---|---|
| deh | veel | studereh |
| de | vil | studere |
| they | will | study |

## They **will be studying**.

### To Study / Studere

**indicative mood:**

| | aspect | |
|---|---|---|
| **tense** | imperfect | perfect |
| past | studerede | havde studeret |
| present | studerer | har studeret |
| future | **vil studere** | vil have studeret |

Jeg **spiser** min frokost inden jeg tager afsted.

| yai | present<br>speese | min | frokost | inden | yai | taghe | afted |
|-----|-------|-----|---------|-------|-----|-------|-------|
| jeg | spiser | min | frokost | inden | jeg | tager | afsted |
| i | eat | my | lunch | before | i | take | away |

I **will have eaten lunch** before I leave.

## To Eat / Spise

indicative mood:

|  | aspect | |
|---|---|---|
| **tense** | imperfect | perfect |
| past | spiste | havde spist |
| present | **spiser** | har spist |
| future | vil spise | vil have spist |

De **vil have ventet** i over en time.

| deh | present<br>veel | infinitive<br>hav | past participle<br>ventet | ee | ower | en | teem |
|-----|-----|-----|-----|-----|-----|-----|-----|
| de | vil | have | ventet | i | over | en | time |
| they | will | have | waited | in | over | an | hour |

They **will have been waiting** for an hour.

## To Wait / Vente

indicative mood:

|  | aspect | |
|---|---|---|
| **tense** | imperfect | perfect |
| past | ventede | havde ventet |
| present | venter | har ventet |
| future | vil vente | **vil have ventet** |

# Thing-Converters

In Danish, thing-converters, also known as prepositions in traditional grammar, are placed before their target thing.

## Jeg går **i** butikken.

| | | thing-converter | thing | |
|---|---|---|---|---|
| yai | goh | **ee** | buteek | en |
| jeg | går | **i** | butik | -en |
| i | go | **in** | store | the |

I go **to** the store.

## Hun går **foran** ham.

| | | thing-converter | thing |
|---|---|---|---|
| hoon | goh | **foh-an** | hahm |
| hun | går | **foran** | ham |
| she | walks | **before** | him |

She walks **in front of** him.

## Den er **i** posen.

| | | thing-converter | thing | |
|---|---|---|---|---|
| den | ehr | **ee** | pos | en |
| den | er | **i** | pos | -en |
| it | is | **in** | bag | the |

It is **in** the bag.

## Vandet er **til** hunden.

| | | | thing-converter | thing | |
|---|---|---|---|---|---|
| van | et | ehr | **til** | hun | en |
| vand | -et | er | **til** | hund | -en |
| water | the | is | **for** | dog | the |

## The water is **for** the dog.

## Bogen er **på** bordet.

| | | | thing-converter | thing | |
|---|---|---|---|---|---|
| bohg | en | ehr | **poh** | bor | eh |
| bog | -en | er | **på** | bord | -et |
| book | the | is | **on** | table | the |

## The book is **on** the table.

## Han går **med** hende.

| | | thing-converter | thing |
|---|---|---|---|
| han | goh | **med** | hen-ne |
| han | går | **med** | hende |
| he | goes | **with** | her |

## He goes **with** her.

# Du er hjemme.

| doo | ehr | **thing** |
|-----|-----|-----------|
| | | hyemmeh |
| du | er | hjemme |
| you | are | **at** home |

## You are **at** home.

# Stolen er **ved** computeren.

| | | | **thing-converter** | **thing** | |
|---|---|---|---|---|---|
| stol | en | ehr | **ved** | computer | en |
| stol | -en | er | **ved** | computer | -en |
| chair | the | is | **by** | computer | the |

## The chair is **by** the computer.

# Vi kørte **fra** lufthavnen til stranden.

| | | **thing-converter** | **thing** | | | | |
|---|---|---|---|---|---|---|---|
| we | kurte | **frah** | luft-hahn | en | til | strahn | en |
| vi | kørte | **fra** | lufthavn | -en | til | strand | -en |
| we | drove | **from** | airport | the | to | beach | the |

## We drove **from** the airport to the beach.

# Aben går **op af** trapperne.

| | | | thing-converter | | thing | |
|---|---|---|---|---|---|---|
| ahp | en | goh | **ohp** | **af** | trappeh | ne |
| ab | -en | går | **op** | **af** | trapper | -ne |
| ape | the | goes | **up** | **of** | stairs | the |

The monkey walks **up** the stairs.

# Filmen er **om** mad.

| | | | thing-converter | thing |
|---|---|---|---|---|
| film | en | ehr | **ohm** | mahd |
| film | -en | er | **om** | mad |
| film | the | is | **about** | food |

The movie is **about** food.

# Musen løber **ind i** labyrinten.

| | | | thing-converter | | thing | |
|---|---|---|---|---|---|---|
| moos | en | lubeh | **ind ee** | labyrynt | en |
| mus | -en | løber | **ind i** | labyrint | -en |
| mouse | the | runs | **into** | labyrinth | the |

The mouse runs **into** the maze.

Flyet flyver **over** os.

| | | | thing-converter | thing |
|---|---|---|---|---|
| flue | et | fluveh | **oweh** | os |
| fly | -et | flyver | **over** | os |
| airplane | the | flies | **over** | us |

The airplane flies **over** us.

Jeg går **efter** showet.

| | | thing-converter | thing | |
|---|---|---|---|---|
| yai | goh | **efteh** | show | et |
| jeg | går | **efter** | show | -et |
| i | goes | **after** | show | the |

I leave **after** the show.

Fiskene er **under** båden.

| | | | thing-converter | thing | |
|---|---|---|---|---|---|
| fiske | ne | ehr | **uhn-er** | boh | en |
| fiske | -ne | er | **under** | båd | -en |
| fish | the | are | **under** | boat | the |

The fish are **under** the boat.

# Scene-Converters

## Scene-Converters used with Complete Scenes

Scene-converters, also known as subordinating conjunctions in traditional grammar terminology, are placed before their target scene. In these examples, the scenes attached to the scene-converter are all complete, meaning they don't have any missing scene components.

### Example #1

In this example, the scene 'she gave him a book' is being used as a thing, specifically a concept. It serves the role of a direct object in the outer scene, 'i thought [something]'.

## Jeg troede, **at hun gav ham en bog**.

| | | scene-converter | subject |
|---|---|---|---|
| jeg | troede | **at** | hun |
| i | thought | **that** | she |

| verv | indirect object | direct object | |
|---|---|---|---|
| gav | ham | en | bog |
| gave | him | a | book |

## I thought **that she gave him a book**.

## Example #2

Here, the scene 'the train will leave' is also being used as a thing, specifically a time. It serves the role of direct object in the outer scene 'he knows [something]'.

### Han ved, **hvornår toget går**.

| | | scene-converter | subject | | verb |
|---|---|---|---|---|---|
| han | ved | **hvornår** | tog | -et | går |
| he | knows | **when** | train | the | goes |

### He knows **when the train will leave**.

## Example #3

The scene 'the treats were hidden' is used as a thing, specifically a place. It serves the role of direct object in the outer scene 'the dog discovered [something]'.

### Hunden opdagede, **hvor godbidderne var gemt**.

| | | | scene-converter |
|---|---|---|---|
| hund | -en | opdagede | **hvor** |
| dog | the | discovered | **where** |

| subject | | verb | |
|---|---|---|---|
| godbidder | -ne | var | gemt |
| treats | the | were | hidden |

### The dog discovered **where the treats were hidden**.

## Scene-Converters used with Incomplete Scenes

Scene-converters can also be used with scenes that have a missing component. In this book, scenes with a missing component are referred to as blanked scenes. Blanked scenes are often used as descriptors of things.

### Example #4

In this example, the blanked scene 'i have read [ ]' is being used as a descriptor for its target thing, 'the book'.

This blanked scene is blanked because it is missing its direct object. If the target thing were written into the blanked scene, it would become the complete scene: 'i have read the book'.

The entire target + descriptor unit, 'the book that i read', plays the role of a subject in the enclosing sentence: '[it] was interesting'.

### Bogen som jeg læste var interessant.

| target | | scene-converter | subject |
|---|---|---|---|
| bog | -en | **som** | jeg |
| book | the | **that** | i |

| verb | | | |
|---|---|---|---|
| læste | var | interessant | |
| read | was | interesting | |

### The book that I read was interesting.

## Example #5

Here, the blanked scene 'we made [ ]' is being used as a descriptor for its target thing, 'the salad'.

This blanked scene is blanked because it is missing its direct object. If the target were written into the blanked scene, it would become the complete scene: 'we made the salad'.

The entire target + descriptor unit 'the salad that we made' plays the role of a direct object in the enclosing sentence: 'he ate [it]'.

### Han spiste **den salat, som vi lavede**.

| | | target | |
|---|---|---|---|
| han | spiste | den | salat |
| he | ate | the | salad |

| scene-converter | subject | verb |
|---|---|---|
| **som** | vi | lavede |
| **that** | we | made |

### He ate **the salad that we made**.

## Example #6

Here, the blanked scene 'she gave me [ ]' is being used as a descriptor for its target thing, 'the box'.

This blanked scene is blanked because it is missing its direct object. Written as a complete scene, the target + descriptor unit would be: 'she gave me the box'.

The entire target + descriptor unit 'the box that she gave me' plays the role of a subject in the enclosing scene: '[it] was green'.

### Kassen som hun gav mig var grøn.

| | target | | scene-converter | subject |
|---|---|---|---|---|
| | kass | -en | **som** | hun |
| | box | the | **that** | she |

| indirect object | | verb | | |
|---|---|---|---|---|
| gav | | mig | var | grøn |
| gave | | me | was | green |

### The box that she gave me was green.

# Practice Sentences

Den grå kat løber stille på hegnet.

| common, singular → | common, singular → | common, singular | present simple |
|---|---|---|---|
| deh | groh | kaht | loobeh |
| den | grå | kat | løber |
| the | gray | cat | run |

| ← descriptor | thing-converter | neuter, singular | neuter, ← singular |
|---|---|---|---|
| steeleh | poh | haign | et |
| stille | på | hegn | -et |
| quietly | on | fence | the |

The gray cat runs quietly on the fence.

Jeg spiser langsomt store kartofler i en time.

| 1st person, singular, nominative | present simple | ← descriptor | common, plural → |
|---|---|---|---|
| yai | speeseh | langsomt | storeh |
| jeg | spiser | langsomt | store |
| i | eat | slowly | big |

| common, plural | thing-converter | common, singular → | common, singular |
|---|---|---|---|
| kartofleh | ee | en | teem |
| kartofler | i | en | time |
| potatoes | in | an | hour |

I slowly eat large potatoes for one hour.

## Hun købte mange gamle malerier fra butikken.

| 3rd person, singular, feminine, nominative | past simple | neuter, plural → | neuter, plural → |
|---|---|---|---|
| hoon | kobte | mange | gamleh |
| hun | købte | mange | gamle |
| she | bought | many | old |

| neuter, plural | thing-converter | common, singular | common, ← singular |
|---|---|---|---|
| malerieh | ee | butik | en |
| malerier | i | butik | -en |
| paintings | in | store | the |

## She bought many old paintings from the store.


## De ti lave mænd hopper lykkeligt over stolen.

| common, plural → | → | common, plural → | common, plural | present simple |
|---|---|---|---|---|
| deh | tee | lehve | men | hoppeh |
| de | ti | lave | mænd | hopper |
| the | 10 | short | men | jump |

| ← descriptor | thing-converter | common, singular | common, ← singular |
|---|---|---|---|
| lek-eh-leeg | oh-eh | stohl | en |
| lykkeligt | over | stol | -en |
| happily | over | chair | the |

## The ten short men jump happily over the chair.

Han tog en tallerken fra opvaskemaskinen og satte den på bordet.

| 3rd person, singular , masculine, nominative | past simple | common, singular → | common, singular |
|---|---|---|---|
| hahn | toh | een | tallerken |
| han | tog | en | tallerken |
| he | took | a | plate |

| thing-converter | common, singular | common, ← singular | present simple |
|---|---|---|---|
| fra | op-vaske-maskine | en | set |
| fra | opvaskemaskine | -en | satte |
| from | dishwasher | the | set |

| 3rd person, singular , common, oblique | thing-converter | neuter, singular | neuter, ← singular |
|---|---|---|---|
| den | poh | bohr | eh |
| den | på | bord | -et |
| it | on | table | the |

He took a plate from the dishwasher and put it on the table.

Manden spiser en lækker chokoladekage.

| common, singular | common, singular | present simple |
|---|---|---|
| man | en | speeseh |
| mand | -en | spiser |
| man | the | eats |

| common singular | common singular | common singular |
|---|---|---|
| een | leikkeh | chokolade-keik |
| en | lækker | chokoladekage |
| a | delicious | chocolate cake |

The man eats a delicious chocolate cake.

# Scene Builder

1) Pick a scene type

   a) Scene comes with empty sockets for subject, verb, and maybe a complement or objects

   b) Pick a process or state to act as the scene's verb


2) Plug pronouns or things into the subject and object sockets

   a) Pronoun - choose its correct spelling based on its perspective, gender, count, and case

   b) Thing - choose its correct spelling based on its count

      i)   Descriptors - choose correct spelling based on target thing's gender and count


3) Decide the verb's mood, tense, and aspect


4) Choose correct spelling of the verb based on mood, tense, and aspect

# I ate a large pizza.

1) [to eat] → **spise**, as transitive
    a) **spise(SBJ, DO)**

2) 2 sockets
    a) SBJ [i] → **jeg**
        i)    Personal Pronoun
                (1) Perspective: 1st person
                (2) Gender: n/a
                (3) Count: singular
                (4) Case: nominative

    b) DO [a large pizza]
        i)    Thing Phrase
                (1) Thing: [pizza] → **pizza**
                    (a) Gender: common
                    (b) Count: singular
                    (c) Article: indefinite article
                (2) Indefinite Article: [a] → **en**
                    (a) Match thing's Gender: common
                    (b) Match thing's Count: singular
                (3) Descriptor: [large] → **stor**
                    (a) Match thing's Gender: common
                    (b) Match thing's Count: singular
                    (c) Article: indefinite article

3) Verb will have
    a) Mood: indicative
    b) Tense: past
    c) Aspect: imperfect

4) Choose spelling of spise for MTA:
    a) MTA = indicative, past, imperfect
    b) spise → **spiste**

5) Danish translation is: **spiste(jeg, en store pizza)**

# Jeg spiste en stor pizza.

Made in the USA
Monee, IL
22 December 2023